Reptiles ~~Follow~~ Break ~~Rules~~

Contents

Written by Isabel Thomas

Collins

Meet the rule breakers

Reptiles have dry, scaly skin. They cannot produce their own body heat.

Lizards are reptiles.

Some reptiles are exceptional. Get ready to meet the reptiles that break rules!

Snakes are reptiles.

Rule 1: Animals can't walk on water

Basilisks dance across water to escape predators! Their back limbs move so fast that a bubble of air forms under each foot. Basilisks push against this bubble to avoid sinking.

Don't try this at home!

Rule breaker:
basilisk

Rule breaker:
pygmy gecko

Pygmy geckos can walk across puddles. This stops them drowning when it rains.

Rule 2: Eyes come in pairs

Some reptiles from New Zealand have three eyes! Their third eye is covered with scales, but scientists know that it can sense light. However, it's not for vision. It helps the reptile know when it's time to breed.

third eye in middle of face

Rule breaker:
New Zealand reptile

This Madagascar blindsnake has no eyes at all!

Rule 3: Animals take in air with their noses

Most animals take in air with their nose and mouth. This river turtle is an exception. It can take in air, using special glands in its bottom! These soak up oxygen from the water, helping the turtle to stay submerged for days.

Rule breaker:
river turtle

Rule 4: Animals use colours to blend in

Many reptiles use colour to blend in with the scenery. But chameleons change colour to stand out!

They change their skin's appearance to attract mates or to scare rivals.

Rule breaker:
chameleon

Rule 5: Animals need limbs to climb

Cave racer snakes have no arms or legs but are excellent climbers. They climb steep cave walls and find a crevice or crack. They dangle from there to catch bats that fly past!

Rule breaker:
cave racer snake

Rule 6: Only insects buzz

This fish-eating crocodile's snout has a knob at the end. The strange appearance is a sign that he is male. He uses it to blow bubbles and produce a buzzing sound. This helps him to attract females.

Rule breaker:
fish-eating crocodile

The crocodile's teeth knit together to help it catch wriggling fish!

Rule 7: Animals can't see in the dark

These pythons have different types of vision. Their eyes can see in the light. Their lips can see in the dark!

Rule breaker:
python

The lips have special receptors that detect heat. Even in total darkness and silence, the snake knows where its prey is hiding.

Rule 8: Missing limbs don't grow back

If a skink is attacked, muscles in its tail pull away from each other and the tail falls off. The wriggling tail acts as a distraction while the skink escapes! The skink grows a new tail to replace the old one.

Scientists have many questions about reptiles. They want to know how reptiles' special features help them to survive. This information could help us to protect reptiles.

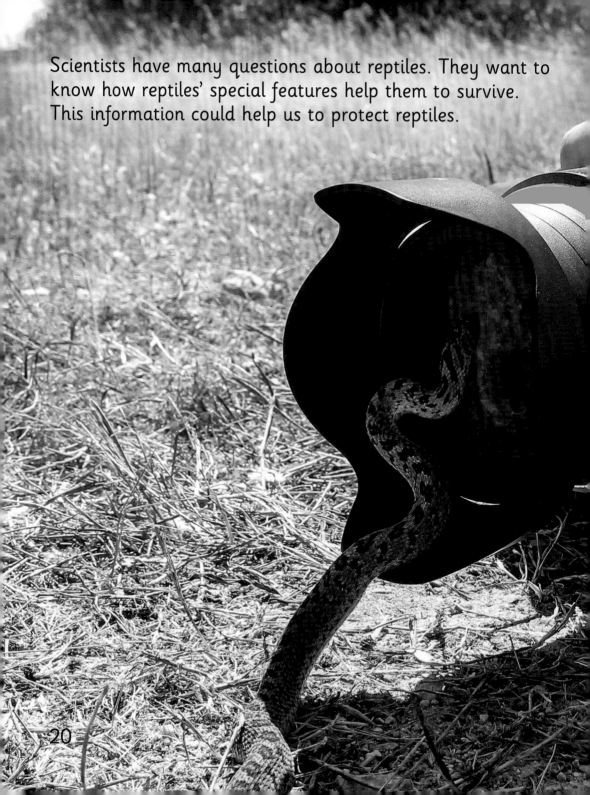

Reptiles

23

After reading

Letters and Sounds: Phase 5–6

Word count: 491

Focus phonemes: /n/ kn, gn /m/ mb /r/ wr /s/ c, ce, sc /c/ x /zh/ sion /sh/ ti, ci

Common exception words: of, to, the, are, one, their, break, water, many, move, eye

Curriculum links: Science: Animals, including humans

National Curriculum learning objectives: Reading/word reading: apply phonic knowledge and skills as the route to decode words; read accurately by blending sounds in unfamiliar words containing GPCs that have been taught; re-read books to build up their fluency and confidence in word reading; Reading/comprehension: discuss word meanings; discuss the significance of the title and events

Developing fluency

- Look at the contents page with your child. Ask your child:
  - What page could I find out about animals that use colour to blend in? (*page 10*)
- Take turns with your child to read a page. Model reading with fluency and expression.

Phonic practice

- Ask your child:
  - Which grapheme makes the /s/ sound in these words: **produce**, **escape**, **crevice**, **dance**, **scientists**? (*produce, escape, crevice, dance, scientists*)
  - Can you identify the suffixes in these words: drowning, covered, darkness, distraction? (*drowning, covered, darkness, distraction*)

Extending vocabulary

- Ask your child:
  - What does the word **protect** mean? (*to look after something*)
  - Can you think of a sentence using the word **protect**? (e.g. *On the pond, the goose protected her goslings.*)
  - How many words can you think of that mean **protect**? (e.g. *defend, shelter, look after, guard, support, care for*)